Linda terBurg's

THE INCREDIBLE BOOK LAUNCH

A DO-IT-YOURSELF MARKETING PLAN WORKBOOK

© **Copyright 2012 by Linda terBurg**

All rights reserved. No part of this book may be reproduced, stored in a retrieval system or transmitted in any form or by any means without prior written permission of the author, except by a reviewer who may quote brief passages in reviews to be printed in a newspaper, magazine, journal, or on-line blog or bookseller.

Exception: Permission is given for those who purchase this workbook to reproduce the Blank Calendar in the Appendix, and the Goal Sheets only. Purchasers do NOT have permission to share these reproduced pages with others.

ISBN-13: 978-1479213771 // ISBN-10: 1479213772

Cover Design by Mary Lois Sanders
Clipart by www.clipart.com and used by permission.

DEDICATION

For Bruce … my love, my friend, my soul-mate. Your vibrato makes my heart sing. You are truly my greatest audience of one. And I am truly yours.

ACKNOWLEDGEMENTS

This project could not have succeeded without the help and support of many people.

To my friend and editor, Mary Lois Sanders, who can do everything well. I thank you from the bottom of my heart and soul for all the editorial brilliance and guidance and for the final design of the cover. This book could not have been done without you and your expertise.

For my fabulous Master Mind Group, Michele Kreider, Mike Kreider, Theresa Kress and Bruce. Your support and encouragement for this book always lets me believe The Master Mind is listening to me, too.

To Mark Newhouse who helped me on my path.

To Lois Wilmoth-Bennett and Joan West who supported my growth as a Marketing Director.

To the many bloggers and chatters who opened up their hearts and souls during all hours of the day and night chatting about all things social media.

CONTENTS

Foreword vii
How to Use this Book viii

Month Nine: 3
   Books I have to read, after I finish this book! 5

Month Eight — Get Known 7
   Check List 8
   Become an Expert 9
   Write Expert Articles: 13
   Post Expert Articles: 15
   Build Your Blog 17
   Build Networks with Authors in Your Area 19

Month Seven — Your Platform 21
   Check List 22
   Determine Your Book's Market & Message 23
   Develop Your Budget 24
   Develop Your Written Goals 26
   Develop a Master Mind Group 36

Month Six — Get Social on the Internet 39
   Check List 40
   Get On Facebook 41
   Get On Twitter 43
   Get On LinkedIn 44
   Get on Pinterest 44
   Set Up Google Alerts 47
   Now is the Time for a Book Trailer 48
   Join Buffer 49

Month Five — More Social Media 51
   Check List 52
   Have Galley's Made 53
   Book Reviewers 53

Find Blogs and Chat Rooms Related to Your Book 58
Begin Planning Your Videos 60
Top video sharing sites 62

Month Four—Lists and More 63
Check List 64
Start Compiling Your Lists 65
Build Your Email List 67
Decide on a Way to Accept Payment 72
Television Opportunities 73
Radio Shows 74
Speaking Opportunities 75
Decide on Your Distribution 77
Ask for Endorsements 78
Send Your Galleys to Reviewers 79
Start Blogging on Blog Sites with Themes Connected to Your Book 81

Month Three—Time for a Press/Media Kit 83
Check List 84
Develop Your Letter head Stationary and Business Cards 85
Develop the Signature on Your Emails 86
Develop Your Press Kit 87
How to Display Your Press/Media Kit 88
The Pitch Letter 89
The Press Release 91
The Author Bio and Picture 93
The Book Cover 95
A List of Ten Questions with Answers: 96

Month Two—A Bit of Everything 99
Check List 100
Get Your Book Trailer and Videos on Video Sharing Sites 101
Keep Your Blogging Going 101
Start Contacting Television Shows, Radio Shows, Opportunities for Speaking
Engagements and Book Signings 102

Month One—Create Anticipation and Excitement 104
    Check List 105
    Develop Your First Newsletter 106
    Get Promotional Material Printed 107
    Ask Blog Sites if You can Have a Blog Tour 107
    Set up the Facebook Fan Page for Your Book 108
    Are You Still Reading? 108

At Publication Date 109
    Check List 110
    Send out Your First Newsletter Announcing the Publication of Your Book 111
    Have an Open House 112
    Send out Press Releases 113
    Ask the Amazon Top Reviewers to Read and Review Your Book 114
    Ask Your Followers/Customers to Write a Review and Post it on Amazon 115
    Enter Contests 116
    Contests and Awards: 117
    Consider Joining Amazon Prime 119
    Spend a Day Enhancing All of Your Pages on Facebook, Twitter, LinkedIn and Amazon 120
    Sign up for Kindlegraph 121
    Now What? 122

Appendix - Calendars 123

Foreword

Congratulations. You've written your book. If you would like to share your book with the world, this workbook will become your bible. Because now starts the hard part—marketing and publicity.

I have presented around the state of Florida and talked about my six month marketing plan. I constantly had to update, update, update as new technology and resources entered the picture daily. This revolution in the publishing industry and the marketing world conceived my nine month plan. There is so much to do BEFORE your book is published.

Most authors don't want to market. They just want to write. This is fine if you aren't concerned about sharing your book with the world. If you are just writing for yourself, your friends and family you won't need all these steps. That's the beauty of self-publishing today. You can write a book and not need to spend thousands of dollars any more to self-publish.

If you are looking for a more global market, you need a plan. But your marketing effort will be time consuming. I suggest at least 45-60 minutes a day. If you don't want to invest the time you can find someone to market your book for you. Or you can find a marketing coach to help you market. If you go this route be sure you know exactly what you are paying for—what outcomes the marketing company or coach can produce.

Even if you are published by a traditional publisher, you will still need to market. Unless you are a well-established, mainstream, big name author, you will need to lead your marketing campaign. Also, many publishing houses will ask you to submit your marketing plan with your novel. They want to know that YOU have a plan.

Remember, if your goal is to be a recognized author, you have to put on your entrepreneurial hat. You are now a business person who needs a business plan. This workbook will be your written plan.

How to Use this Book

The goal of this book is to count down the months before you publish your book. Since you must start your marketing effort 9 months before your publication date, I start with *Month Nine*. That is what you should try to accomplish nine months before your publication date. Then go to month eight and so on until you reach the publication month.

If you have already published your book and need a plan now, don't fret. It is never too late. Take the most important pieces of each month and start them now. If your book is over one or two years old, consider bringing it out again. Can you write a revision which makes it new? Be creative.

This book is laid out with the monthly plan on the first page of each chapter. The following pages in the chapter give you ways to accomplish each task. Usually, there is one page per task. Because this is a workbook, check off your accomplishments with the date they are completed. You will find a spot or two empty each month to add any additional marketing activities you feel are particularly important for your individual plan. There is a place for notes.

This plan is not set in stone. Every book is different and a cookie cutter plan may not work for you. However, it can give you the framework you need to improvise your own plan. The plan each month will list a first (1), second (2) and third (3) activity I feel are the most important. If you do anything for that month, these activities would be my choices.

At the back of this book there will be an example of a nine month marketing plan outlining each month using calendars. I took the month of December as my publication date and backed up nine months with all the planning. I have included a blank calendar which you are permitted to reproduce. Put in your expected publication date and back up nine months with the start of your reading. Of course, if you are really ambitions, you can start your planning even a year before or 18 months before. Some people believe you should start planning three years before your book is published.

Good luck. I know how talented my writer friends are and, with targeted marketing, I'm sure your talents will exceed your dreams. Now is your opportunity.

> "Opportunity is missed by most people because it's dressed in overalls and looks like work."
> Thomas Alva Edison

Marketing Requires Commitment

****

Making Connections
Is the Essence
Of Marketing

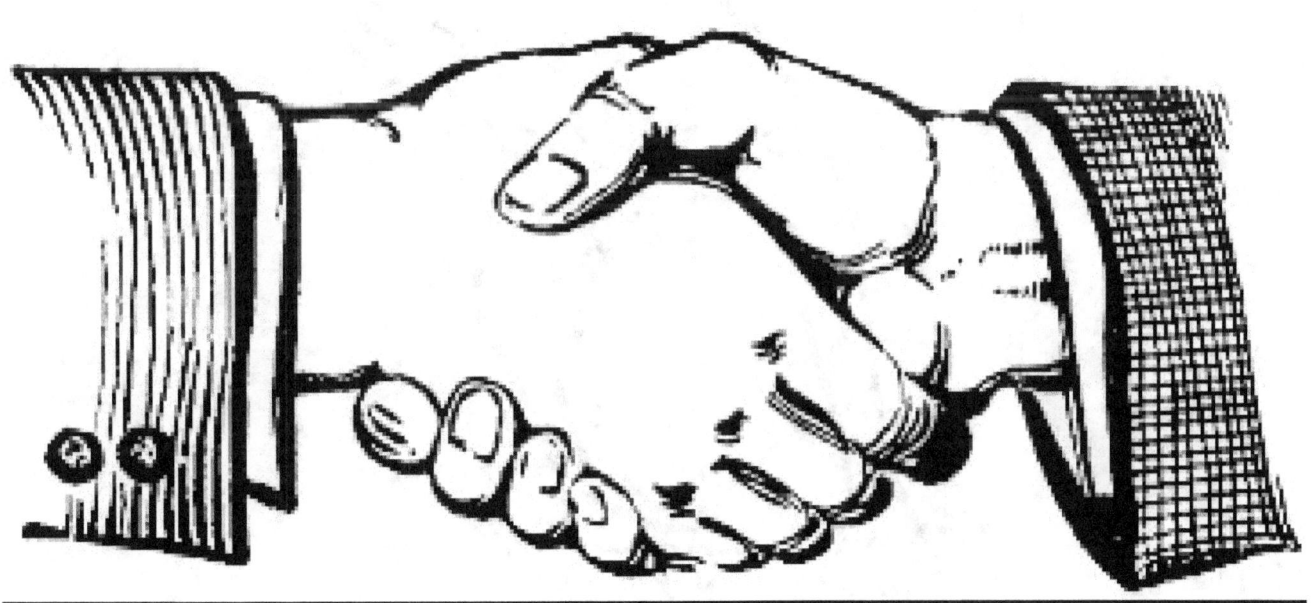

The Question is not
***Should* you Market?**

But *How* you should you Market.

You can no longer bury your head in the sand.

Month Nine:
The Countdown Begins: A Time to Read

This is your month to read, Read, READ. I will not put an exclamation mark there as much as I would like to. While attending a seminar with author Steve Berry, he said we shouldn't use them in our writing. Not even in our emails.

I am providing your reading list in the first chapter since I want you to start reading now. Read even while you are finishing your manuscript. But first, you need to read this book, **The Incredible Book Launch,** from cover to cover. Some books you can borrow from the library, some you must buy and some are free.

Again, please make sure that you read this book first in its entirety. By doing this you should get a good feel for where you are headed each month and why.

Notes

Books I have to read, after I finish this book!

1. *1001 Ways to Market Your Books*. John Kremer. Open Horizons. http://www.bookmarket.com - A must have.

2. *Independent Consulting*. David Kintler with Bob Adams. Adams Media Corporation. www.adamsmedia.com

3. *Plug Your Book*. Steve Weber. Weber Books. www.weberbooks.com - Great for internet marketing.

4. *Marketing Kit for Dummies*. Alexander Hiam. www.amazon.com/books

5. *Writer's Market*. Writer's Digest Books. - Get the latest edition. You can even check older editions out of the library since they also have good articles. www.writersdigestshop.com

6. *6 Steps to Free Publicity*. Marcie Yudkin. Career Press, Inc.

7. *The Creative Writer's Notebook*. www.courtjesterpublications.com - Great writing tips, workshops, events and contest information. Mary Lois Sanders, editor. Monthly newsletter.

8. *The Frugal Book Promoter: How to Do What your Publisher Won't*. Carolyn Howard-Johnson. A Star Publish Book.

9. *Facebook Marketing for Dummies*. Paul Dunay and Richard Krueger. Wiley Publishing, Inc.

10. *Power Friending: Demystifying Social Media to Grow Your Business*. Amber Mac. Penguin Group.

11. *Blogging All-In-One for Dummies: 8 Books in 1*. Susan Gunelius

12. *Self-Publishing Manual: How to Write, Print and Sell Your Own Book*. Dan Poynter

Notes

Month Eight—Get Known

Your goal this month is to make your presence known in the social media. You are not selling books here, but establishing yourself as a presence on the internet.

Check List

- _____ Become an expert (1)

- _____ Write expert articles

- _____ Explore article directories listed in this book

- _____ Post articles on article directories

- _____ Build your blog not your website (2)

- _____ Build networks with other authors in your area or through Skype (3)

- _____

- _____

- _____

- _____

Become an Expert

First, you must believe you are already an expert in something. You have written a book and gathered a lot of information. Think about the experts you know. Do you really know where their expertise comes from? Do they have a degree in that subject? You probably don't know. List 10 experts you know who are able to talk intelligently about their subjects. Do the same thing with your knowledge. Create your image as the go-to person.

1. _____In the boxes on page 11, write down 8 things from your book you can talk about as an expert. If you are writing a novel, what other nonfiction subjects could you include? Does your book include divorce? Adoption? Was one of the characters autistic? Start thinking outside the box.

2. _____Do an Internet search for these 8 things and find other articles about these topics.

3. _____Identify experts in your field and interview them. Write down two experts you could interview:

    - _____
    - _____

4. _____Read articles about these topics at the article directories listed in this chapter. What kinds of questions are people asking? Answer those questions. Make yourself the go-to person when you write your articles. Four questions people are asking are:

    - _____
    - _____
    - _____

5. _____There is a book called *How to Become an Expert on Anything in Less than Two Hours* by Gregory Hartley and Maryann Karinch. It gives some good ideas you can latch onto. It is available at on-line bookstores.

Notes

I am an expert in these categories.
I am the go-to person.

Notes

Write Expert Articles:

1. _____Write expert articles.

2. _____Try for at least one a week in the beginning.

3. _____To supplement your articles, you can download private label rights articles (PLR) for free or buy them from other writers.

You may write expert articles by yourself or you can do an Internet search for "PLR articles." These articles are free with private label rights. You can use them any way you would like.

Rewrite these articles so that your copy will be new and fresh. The search engines will like this article better and send more search engines to the article if it is fresh. You can also buy articles other people have written.

It's thought that when you write your article or rewrite your PLR article **keyword density** is very important. Search engine spiders scan a page in a way that makes it important to place your keywords where they will be detected. That way your article will come up when someone searches for it.

What is keyword density? It is how many times your keyword is placed in your article. Today there is a tool which provides a good yardstick for using key words.

Your article might get more hits if you do an Internet search for the questions searchers are looking for. Use the program www.googlekeywordtool.com and enter the key words you believe people use. You will get a breakdown of how many words and phrases are used by the searchers each month.

When you enter the site, type in a word that searchers might use to find your article and see how it ranks.

Words and phrases that are used most by searchers to find my articles are:

- _____
- _____
- _____

Notes

Post Expert Articles:

1. _____Post your articles on the sites listed below. Explore the article directories located below. Find out the requirements for article placement and follow the instructions. If you only post on one site use **ezinearticles.** That site is probably the most read.

Article Directory Sites

- www.vretoolbar.com "Over 100 Niche Content Website Tools at Your Fingertips"
- www.ehow.com
- www.squidoo.com
- www.ezinearticles.com
- www.suite101.com (new changes coming)

End each Article with:

- ____ A great biography
- ____Titles of your books
- ____Links where to find you
- ____Social media links (Facebook, LinkedIn, etc.) Remember, people are free to repost your articles on these social media sites.

Article Sites I will use for posting my articles:

- _____
- _____
- _____
- _____

Notes

Build Your Blog

_____ Build your Blog - Many of you already have an up and running blog or website. If you don't, now is the time to get it. This is especially important now since you are putting your articles on the internet. But it is even more important to turn your website into a blog. With a blog you can actually develop relationships with your customers. It is interactive. Mike Stelzner, Social Media Examiner (mike@socialmediaexaminer.com) says, "Businesses with blogs get 55% more traffic."

Build relationships with your blogging. The most important pieces of blogging are:

- Good content
- Good conversation
- Timely responses. Get back to people right away when they comment.
- A standardized time frame of writing. Will you write once a day, once a week? Stay consistent.

Make sure your blog captures attention and drives customers to it. You can create your blog yourself or have a professional create one for you.

It is important to have a landing page on your blog since you are trying to sell books. Then, when people read an article you have written, they click on your link and they go directly to your blog, landing on the landing page.

Your **landing page** should include:

- _____A place to ask for their email address for your list
- _____Something you are giving away for free. This could be an article or a short book you have written. Ask for their email address and in return send a download.
- _____An offer to send a monthly email full of tips.
- _____A way to advertise your books and a way for the customer to buy the books.

Notes

Build Networks with Authors in Your Area

Don't be afraid to build networks and partnerships with other authors. I live in Florida and would certainly love to build networks with authors in The Writers League of The Villages, Florida and The Florida Writers Association. Build up an affiliation with these authors. You might write articles about each other and include links which link your pages together. You can feature each other on blog tours or go in together for resource materials. You can get into the same groups on LinkedIn and guide some conversations.

You might go further and decide to represent each other to outside sources. Once, when I was working as the marketing director to a small publisher, I was talking to a radio show host/author who wanted to feature my author on his program. After we talked for awhile, he asked about my representing him. He said he liked how I promoted my author and would like someone to speak for him. I believe you could work with an author's affiliation and speak for each other.

Go to authors you know in the area and suggest an affiliation. Talk to authors you know through local writers' groups or state level groups. You have nothing to lose and everything to gain.

List 6 authors you could contact to form an affiliation:

- _____
- _____
- _____
- _____
- _____
- _____

Some ideas we might collaborate on are:

- _____Placing links on each other's blogs
- _____Invite each other for blog tours
- _____Collaborate on article writing
- _____Join the same groups on LinkedIn
- _____Buy resources together
- _____Hold book signings as a group and have a panel discussion
- _____Speak for each other

Notes

Month Seven—Your Platform

This is the month I want you to focus on your marketing plan and goals. These things will drive everything else in your publicity.

Check List

- _____ Determine your book's market and message (2)

- _____ Develop your budget (3)

- _____ Develop your goals (1)

- _____ Consider setting up a Master Mind group

- _____ Read other books similar to your book

- _____ Write reviews on other books like yours on Amazon or other book review sites

- _____

- _____

- _____

- _____

Determine Your Book's Market & Message

Wheatmark® has a marketing plan call the *Book Marketecture* which is very good for identifying your book's market and message. It is **free** as long as you download it yourself. This is a 92 page resource guide. (www.wheatmark.com/BookMarketecture.pdf)

Since I am going to guide you through goal setting later in this section, I would like you start on page 17 with "Identifying Your Book's Key Marketing Message."

There is a lot of information in those 19 pages which will allow you to answer the question of your customer, e.g., "What's in it for me." "Why should I buy your book?"

When you have finished Chapter 2, progress to Chapter 3. This chapter will help you identify your book's key markets.

My book will help you develop a nine month timetable for marketing your book. However, plan out into the future once those months have lapsed and your book is finally published. What will you continue to do and how much time will you be able to devote daily, weekly or monthly on marketing? We will talk about that toward the end of the book.

Develop Your Budget

**Once again you cannot
bury your head in the sand.**

**You must face this with your
Eyes wide open**.

You had to determine a budget for writing your book and sending your book to publishers. Or if you self-published, you had to determine how much you would pay for editing, formatting, publishing and so on. Now you must determine how much you are willing to invest in getting your book out there.

There are many ways to develop a budget. When I did my MBA at Wayne State they were very specific that you MUST have a budget and even gave a percentage of revenue you should spend depending on your industry. So let's talk about a few ways you can determine your budget.

1. **No Money—No Budget**. This is one way of determining how much money you will spend. None! There are many free things out there, but you should be aware that you will be spending anyway. Spending in time, that is. Whenever you use the free stuff you will be investing your time. So determine your time spent and the bang for the buck.

   You might say you will get all your advertising from word of mouth. I love word of mouth and feel this is legitimate. Let's say you start a cupcake business and cater to the neighborhood parties. Pretty soon the word spreads about how wonderful your cupcakes are and people from the next town call you to cater. This happens a couple more times. But pretty soon your luck will run out. This type of campaign will eventually stop growing. Even with word of mouth, you should have a specific plan and dollar amount allocated for marketing.

2. **Zero Balance Budget or Blank Page**. Start with a blank page and begin estimating your costs. Develop your budget from the ground up. This is also called The Flat Dollar Approach.

3. **What you can Afford**. Simply decide how much money you have to invest and do it.

4. **Plan by Your Goals**. When you write your goals, estimate your dollar amount for each goal. If you want to place four ads in the Sunday paper, how much will each ad cost? Do this for every goal you write.

5. **Percentage of Revenue or Net Sales.** If you don't have a sales track record yet, you can estimate this. Then decide what percentage of your sales you will spend on your budget. I've seen a variety of percentages from 7% to 10% of your net sales should be spent on marketing. So if your net sales are $100,000 then $7,000 to $10,000 should be spent on marketing.

6. **Price Ratio to Earnings.** As your sales grow you might want to consider figuring out this ratio (ROI) to determine your marketing budget. There is a site that has a free ROI calculator you can use: www.pine-grove.com .

Develop Your Written Goals

I believe this is one of the most important pieces of your plan. I CANNOT STRESS ENOUGH THE IMPORTANCE OF WELL WRITTEN GOALS TO DRIVE YOUR MARKETING PLAN.

If you have nothing to aim at, you are sure to hit your target.

Your goals must be written. Many people set goals but only about 5% of the people reach them. That 5% have written their goals down and reviewed them on a periodic basis. I believe this is a very powerful piece of information.

The act of writing down your goals actually sets the process in motion. When you write them down there are three things to keep in mind:

1. Review your goals frequently. Write them down, post them on your bathroom mirror, or keep them in your wallet.

2. Write in the positive. When I was in education we would write "Keep your hands down at your sides." We would not write "Don't hit anyone."

3. Be sure your goals are measurable. You must have the yardstick so you can see where you are and where you are headed.

****

Things may come to those who wait,
but only the things left behind by those that hustle.
Abraham Lincoln

****

Whether you believe you can do a thing or not, you are right.
Henry Ford

You must write both **goals** and **benchmarks.** The goal is where you want to be, a broad statement of what you hope to accomplish.

The **benchmarks** (or objectives) are the steps that are needed to get there. They are your pathway. When your benchmarks are completed you move toward your goal.

> **Measurable objectives (benchmarks) state**
>
> - Who is involved?
> - What are the desired outcomes?
> - How is progress measured?
> - When will the outcome occur?

Start scribbling some ideas for goals. Firm up the pieces to the goals when you use the goal writing forms on the next page. Focus not only on the book you have written, but also on your writing career. Put some of your ideas on the next page.

What one goal might you write that could change your life forever? Some ideas are?

The following page has an example of a goal using the goal form.

1. In the **first box** write your broad goal.

2. In the **second box** write the parts of the objective.

3. In the **third box** write the completed objective.

4. In the **fourth box** see if your goal meets these criteria:

   - Specific?
   - Measurable?
   - Time bound?

EXAMPLE

Goal (Broad Statement):

Send my press kit out

Objective #1

Who: I will

What: Send my press kit out to interview contacts

How: Through the mail

When: During the next 3 months

Proficiency level: Ten kits will be sent by (put in the date)

Written Objective:

I will send ten press kits through the mail to interview contacts during the next three months. This objective will be finished on this date:_____

Evaluation:

Specific __yes__   Measurable __yes__   Time-bound __yes__

Goal (Broad Statement):

Objective #1
Who:
What:
How:
When:
Proficiency level:

Written Objective:
_____
_____
_____
_____

Evaluation:
Specific _____   Measurable _____   Time-bound _____

Goal (Broad Statement):

Objective #1

Who:

What:

How:

When:

Proficiency level:

Written Objective:

_____
_____
_____
_____

Evaluation:

Specific _____   Measurable _____   Time-bound _____

Goal (Broad Statement):

Objective #1

Who:

What:

How:

When:

Proficiency level:

Written Objective:
_____
_____
_____
_____

Evaluation:

Specific _____   Measurable _____   Time-bound _____

Goal (Broad Statement):

Objective #1

Who:

What:

How:

When:

Proficiency level:

Written Objective:

_____
_____
_____
_____

Evaluation:

Specific _____   Measurable _____   Time-bound _____

Notes

Develop a Master Mind Group

I love Master Mind Groups. I have been involved with them since the 70s and never had more success as when I was participating in a group. I usually met with 3-4 people on a weekly or bi-weekly basis. In today's world you can even meet with people via conference call on Skype. This is only one good reason to have Skype on your computer. Each person writes his/her goals and then reads them aloud. You can talk about what steps you're taking to meet your goals. The other members in the group support you in your goals. It's that easy.

Master Mind Groups were first developed by Napoleon Hill, the author of *Think and Grow Rich* which was published in the 1920s. Napoleon Hill says a Master Mind group is the "coordination of knowledge and effort of two or more (like minded individuals) who work toward a definite purpose in the spirit of harmony."

You can order a Master Mind journal through Renaissance Unity church in Warren, Michigan (www.renaissanceunity.org). The church prints a new journal yearly. This is a day by day, month by month journal that will cover one calendar year. Throughout the journal there are wonderful words of encouragement such as "I know the master has heard you and is providing what you have asked for."

Here are some positive affirmations that also work with this group:

- I love my writing career so much that it is easy for me to write.
- I have the power to make the changes I need to make in my writing career.
- I move past all limitations into a no-limit life. I achieve my goals easily.
- I attract success and prosperity.

I was investigating a major New York marketing plan and there it was again—The Master Mind group. This New York plan included having you participate in a Master Mind group, with written goals and objectives. I believe they are correct. It's worth bringing back again. Please take time to explore this option and order the journal. You will need to find others to participate in the group with you.

Step to take for a Master Mind Group:

1. _____ Invite 2-4 like-minded people to join a Master Mind Group. Here are the names of the people I will invite.

   _____
   _____
   _____

2. _____Order your Master Mind journals from Unity Church
   www.renaissanceunity.org/mmj.htm

3. _____Set up a day and time to meet. A good time would be
   _____

Notes

Read Books Similar to Your Own:

Go to Amazon and do a search for books that are similar to yours. If I were to do that I would search for books on how to market your novel. Find five books that are similar to yours and write them here.

- _____

- _____

- _____

- _____

- _____

Order those books either hard/soft cover or the e-book version. If you are using The Nook you can order them from Barnes and Nobles. You can also see if your library has these books. Some libraries also have e-books that are available for rent.

Go to Amazon and scroll down to the bottom of the page of one of those books. There is a spot where it says "Write a Review." That is where you give a thoughtful review of the competition. It is another good way to get your name "out there" and to position yourself as an expert.

I will write and post reviews for these books:

- _____ (date)_____

- _____ (date)_____

- _____ (date)_____

Month Six — Get Social on the Internet

There are 800 million active users of social media and 50% of them log in daily. There is also a great increase of people who are using their mobile devices to access the social media. There are 250 million people accessing Facebook through these mobile devices. These statistics grow every day. There is an explosion of social media and you need to be on the boat.

Check List

- _____Get on Facebook (1)

- _____Get on Twitter

- _____Get on LinkedIn (4)

- _____Get on Pinterest

- _____Set up Google Alerts (3)

- _____Make a book trailer or have someone make one for you (2)

- _____Join Buffer (www.bufferapp.com)

- _____

- _____

Get On Facebook

The question now is not *whether* you should get on Facebook. The question is *when* you will get on Facebook. Set up your Facebook personal page so you can develop your Fan Page at a later date. This seems overwhelming to some, but once you get your personal page set there are books to help you with your Fan Page. The personal profile and the fan page are two different pages. I used the Dummy book which gave me all the info I needed to set up my Facebook Fan Page.

By getting on Facebook now, you will begin collecting email addresses of friends, relatives and fans. During "Month One" in this book you will set up your Fan Page on Facebook. This will be a good time to introduce your book and start collecting fans. Ask your "friends" on your Facebook page to visit your Fan Page and click the button to "like" you. Invite them to invite their friends also.

Here's how you get on Facebook:

- _____Go to www.facebook.com

- _____Fill in the "sign up" form on this page

- _____Click "sign up"

- _____You are a member

- _____Upload a photo for your "wall"

- _____Find friends

- _____Send a message

It is important to be on Facebook. If you click on the statistics page you will find some of these statistics for 2011:

- Over 500 million users

- 250 million of these users log in every day

- 72% of all Internet users are on Facebook

Facebook announced in 2012 that it has an audience of 955 million and is closing in on one billion participants

Notes

Get On Twitter

Just like Facebook, set up a Twitter account. You can link both of your accounts. I don't use Twitter very much, but a lot of people like the contacts they make. If you decide to use Twitter, read some of the free manuals about marketing on Twitter. You can do an Internet search for them.

Find people on Twitter with whom you would like to be friends. It might be another author who writes books like yours. It might be a person familiar with the publishing business. Ask that person to join you.

Get On LinkedIn

I really like LinkedIn. It is a great way to make connections with others who have similar interests. I believe you should accept all invitation to connect. If you've heard about the six degrees of separation, you will realize you never know who someone else is connected with.

Also, you should join and follow any of the groups that are pertinent to your expertise or interests. These groups are great sounding boards. Spend a few weeks following the discussions and then post in the question and answer sections. Again, this gets your name out there. People will begin to recognize you. Ask your writing friends to join the same groups so you can all answer questions on the chats.

Get on Pinterest

According to Pinterest, they are "a virtual pinboard, which allows you to organize and share all beautiful things you find on the web." It is very visual.

It is a new social media site that uses boards, pictures and pins. You must be referred to Pinterest by a member or you can go to www.pinterest.com and request an invitation. I requested an invitation and in about 1-2 weeks later there was an email in my inbox welcoming me.

Why should you get on Pinterest? According to their statistic page:

- There are a million visitors every day

- Users have an average household income of $100,000.

- It has grown to one of the top 10 niche sites in one year

Here's how to use Pinterest:

- _____Go to Pinterest

- _____Ask for an invitation

- _____Invite or find friends

- _____Upload your photo

- _____Pull the Pinterest "pin it" button up to your bookmarks bar. They have a video in the help section that shows you how to do this.

- _____Use the "pin it" button to grab an image from any website and pin it to one of your boards

- _____Pin up a picture of your book cover. Pin your affiliates' book covers. Have them pin yours.

- _____Pin up pictures of things associated with your book. A crying baby? A picture of a new recipe? An animal in your book? Get creative.

- _____Put in a great write-up

Go to www.skillshare.com and look for classes on Pinterest. I have signed up with Christin Martinex for "Pinning with a Purpose: Tell Your Story on Pinterest." This class is usually $10.00 but she sometimes offers it for free. Skillshare calls itself a "community marketplace" that makes it easy to teach and take classes.

Here are some ideas for a Pinterest Bulletin Board:

Set Up Google Alerts

To set up your Google Alerts, go to www.Google.com/alerts. Enter key words that you would like to be alerted to. I have set up my name, the name of my book and the words "book marketing." Once a day I get alerts to my email if any of these targeted items appear on the internet. You need to know who is talking and what they are saying. They may even be talking about you or your book.

Set up your Own Alerts:

- _____ Go to the website www.Google.com/alerts

- _____ Enter your name as a search criterion

- _____ Enter the name of your book as a search criterion

- _____ Enter one or two subjects that pertain to your book as a search criterion. I wouldn't enter any more since you will be getting alerts almost daily and you don't want too much to read.

- _____ The subjects I will enter as search criterion are:

1. _____

2. _____

> "The only thing worse than people talking about you is people not talking about you."
> Oscar Wilde

Now is the Time for a Book Trailer

So what is a book trailer? It is a short video, about 1.5-2 minutes that hooks the reader and creates a desire to read your book. Go to YouTube and search "Book Trailers" and you will find many. If you do an Internet search for "Book Trailer" you will find many companies that will make them for you. The prices for this service vary greatly. You can even go to www.fiverr,com and find someone to make one for you for $5.00.

I remember, though, what my father taught me: "In this life, you only get what you pay for." You want a book trailer that will cause some buzz. You would like people to see your trailer and watch it again. Or forward it to someone else because it is well done and clever.

Post your video on YouTube, other video sharing sites and on your blog or website. You can embed it in an article you are writing to give further information about the article.

- _____Go to YouTube and search "book trailers." Watch these as you plan your own.

- _____ Do an Internet search for "book trailers" and you will find companies that will make your book trailers for you.

- _____Start sketching out what you would like to be included in your trailer.

- _____Make your book trailer.

- _____Post your book trailer on YouTube and other video sharing sites I have listed in this book, or have a book trailer company do this for you.

Join Buffer

Buffer is a great app that sends posts to Facebook, Twitter and LinkedIn at the same time. You can set up your own posts or you can browse their posts. After you write your posts you can schedule your release to these social media sites. So spend 30 minutes setting up your posts for the next few days and you can forget about posting for a day or two.

Even if you use Buffer, it is important you connect with your audience and respond to their posts. You really need to connect on a regular basis and keep new information in the forefront.

Buffer has a new program that will automatically set the best times Twitter suggests for releasing your tweets.

There is another new program in Twitter called "Click to Tweet." Twitter says it's "the best, easiest and simplest way to promote and advertise in Twitter." You go to click to tweet, write your message in the box, click "Generate" button to create a custom link such as your blog landing page and then share the page. Whoever clicks on the link has that message added to their status box.

I have:

- _____Joined Buffer

- _____Set Buffer tweets for Twitter using their suggested times

- _____Set other messages for Facebook

Notes

Month Five — More Social Media

Check List

- _____Have galleys made (This is not social media. But you must do it here.)

- _____Find blogs and chat rooms relating to your book (1)

- _____Begin planning the 1st of 10 short videos for video sharing sites (2)

- _____Get a list of video sharing sites available (Some are available in this chapter)

- _____ _____

- _____ _____

Have Galley's Made

Make galleys so you can send a copy of your book to reviewers. Most reviewers want your book sent to them 3-4 months before the publication date and they want unbound galleys. When I worked for the publishing company they maneuvered this date somewhat. It isn't necessarily the date your book is printed, but the date you have listed for these prepublication reviewers. You can sell books before the publication date.

You can have your galleys done online by doing an Internet search or you can go to your local Staples and have a galley made of your book. Below, I have included a list of reviewers you might want to send your book to. Go to each reviewer's website and read the guidelines for submission.

Besides the prepublication book reviewers, you can ask magazines for reviews. If you have a book on ADD find the magazines that cover this topic and might be interested in reviewing your book. You can do this after the publication date.

Book Reviewers

Having your book reviewed by a major reviewer can help sell your book. You can also use the review as a great PR tool on your website, blog and social networking sites. It's a small investment for a big bang for your money.

1. **Booklist, American Library Association**: 50 E. Huron St., Chicago, IL 60611; http://www.ala.org/booklist. Send bound galleys a few months before launch (15 weeks in most cases.) Check website on whom to address and what to send.

2. **Kirkus Reviews:** Go to the website for submission guidelines. http://www.kirkusreviews.com They also have a program called Kirkus Indie where you can pay for a review.

3. **Library Journal**: Go to the website for submission guidelines. http://libraryjournal.com

4. **Newsday**: www.newsday.com For book reviews call (631) 843-4659 or email tom.beer@newsday.com

5. **New York Review of Books**: Send all books to Robert Silvers, the magazine's editor. The New York Review of Books, 435 Hudson Street, Suite 300, New York, NY 10014. See http://wwwnybooks.com.

6. **New York Times**: Galleys of books for review-consideration should be sent three to four months in advance of publication. If galleys are not available, the finished book may be sent. Familiarize yourself with books they do and do not review. Send to "Editor of the Book Review", The New York Times Book Review, 620 Eighth Avenue, 5th Floor, New York NY 10018. Children's books go to Children's Book Editor. See http://www.nytimes.com

7. **Romantic Times**: Send galleys/manuscripts to the appropriate reviewer four months prior to your book's publication date. Check the website for all submission guidelines. See http://www.rtbookreviews.com.

8. **The Author's Review:** Renee Bobb, Renee Bobb Media Group, P.O. Box 583, Hermitage, TN 37076. This is a TV talk show. The best way to pitch the program is to mail Renee a copy of your book, information about your topic, include your press kit, and provide a brief description of how you will help market the show.

9. **Historical Novels Review:** Go to website; click on "submit a book for review." http://www.historicalnovelsociety.org.

10. **BookPage**: www.bookpage.com. Send advance copy 3 months prior to publication date. If no galleys are available, send a finished book ASAP. Cannot consider a book for review if received after publication date. Check website for where to send adult titles and children's titles.

11. **New York Journal of Books**: Click on "Review Requests" at the bottom of the page. www.nyjournalofbooks.com

12. **Publisher's Weekly:** Considers self-published books through PW Select Program explained in their submission guidelines. www.publishersweekly.com/pw/corp/submissionguidelines.html

Book Reviewers I will Send my Book to:

- _____
- _____
- _____
- _____
- _____

Paste your reviews here.

Here are the awesome things people have said about my book:

More great things people have said about my book:

Find Blogs and Chat Rooms Related to Your Book

Do an Internet search to find blogs and chat rooms related to your book. Spend time searching for blogs and explore the conversations. Although I've listed a site for chatting, you will do best if you do an Internet search for the name of your topic and the words "chat room." Once you get the hang of the conversations start making yourself known. Don't just be a stalker. Join the conversations.

Don't chat for the sole purpose of selling your book. Look at the questions chatters are asking. Can you help them? Track the kinds of questions people are asking. This could be the sequel to your current book. Above all, build relationships. Remember, that is the core of marketing.

Some sites for locating chat rooms are:

- www.messenger.yahoo.com
- www.technorati.com
- www.alltop.com
- www.blogcatalog.com
- www.big-boards.com
- www.groups.google.com

When you find a site that pertains to your book, write that site here for future reference. Also, bookmark these sites on your computer.

- _____
- _____
- _____
- _____
- _____
- _____

Become chat room savvy with these acronyms:

- AAK — Alive and Kicking
- AFK — Away From the Keyboard
- B4 — Before
- BBL — Be Back Later
- CU — See You
- IDK or IDN — I don't know
- IMO — In My Opinion
- LOL — Laugh Out Loud
- LMAO — Laughing My Ass Off
- NP — No Problem
- BTW — By The Way
- SH — Same Here
- TAFN — That's All For Now
- TNX — Thanks
- TTYL — Talk To You Later
- YW — You're Welcome

Begin Planning Your Videos

Plan the videos you release to video sharing sites. Determine your schedule for video releasing. You might want to release a video a week or one every other week. Most of these sites will share your video for free. You just need to produce it and download it to the site.

These videos will create your presence on the internet. Here are some ideas for videos:

- Have one video explaining why you wrote this book.
- One talking about the research you did for the book.
- Have one of your readers give an endorsement for your book. Show his/her picture and record his/her voice talking about your book.
- Develop one "how to" video. How to sell something or how to improve your health. Use expert knowledge from your book.

"How To" videos are the most watched videos on the internet. Determine if you can put one or two "how to" videos into your selection. I believe this is very important.

Release your videos to the video sharing sites listed on page 62. New sites develop every day, so you can do an Internet search for "video sharing sites" and see what else is available.

If you are producing your own videos, do an Internet search for tips on how to produce a good video. Remember, your videos should be relatively short, only about a minute and a half. Write out your script and try to keep it to a paragraph or two. Get a hook. Something the audience will remember. Remember to have good lighting and sound. You will probably look best if you film inside. Outside lighting is not as flattering.

Check out a new product called "Swivl.". It is like having your own camera man. Put your iPhone into the device, attach a remote to your shirt and the camera follows you around. Much more interesting than only a boring head shot. At this writing it is less than $200. Go to www.swivl.com.

Some ideas for my 1½-minute videos are:

- _____
- _____
- _____
- _____

At least one of my videos is a "how to" video.

Top video sharing sites

1. Google video
2. Bright Cove
3. Photo Bucket
4. YouTube
5. Daily Motion
6. Zippy Videos
7. Clipmoon
8. Blip.tv
9. GrindTV
10. Myspace
11. Vimeo
12. ThatsHow
13. LiveLeak
14. Stupidvideos
15. MeraVideo
16. Tubetorial
17. Kwego
18. Lulu
19. Pandora
20. Viddler
21. Putfile
22. Vmix
23. Dotv
24. Gawkk
25. GoFish
26. Flixya
27. Vidmax
28. Break
29. BuzzNet
30. iFilm

Month Four—Lists and More

Check List

- _____Begin compiling your lists—Radio, email, TV, speaker opportunities (1)

- _____Decide on a way to accept credit cards

- _____Decide on your distribution (Amazon? Barnes and Noble? Your web page?)

- _____Ask people for endorsements for your book

- _____Send galleys to reviewers

- _____Start blogging on blog sites related to you book (2)

- _____

- _____

Start Compiling Your Lists

Each list you compile will be different. Have one for television, one for radio, one for emails and one for speaking opportunities.

Here are some books that give information about the news media:

- Gale Directory of Publications and Broadcast Media

- The Standard Periodical Directory

- Burrelle's Media Directory - www.burrellesluce.com

- Bacon's Media Directory

- The Standard Periodical Directory

- Ulrich's International Periodicals Directory

- Gebby Press - www.gebbieinc.com

Notes

Build Your Email List

Now is the time to start collecting names and emails for your newsletters and press releases. You can:

- Invite your friends, relatives, family and other fans to join your list.

- Ask friends if they have anyone they know who would like to join your list.

- When you speak, be sure to find a way to collect email addresses. Ask their permission to send them something free and put them on your email list. Have a card they will fill out.

I must be clear when I say "with their permission." The laws are tough on spamming. Spamming is sending emails to people who did not ask to be on your list. When I worked with Constant Contact they shut down our email newsletter because there were too many spam reports. I had to completely rework our email list to be certain everyone on the list requested our newsletter.

You can also build your email list by putting something free on the landing page of your blog. Find something to give away. It could be a periodic newsletter. You are asking for their permission to email them for the giveaway and for future emails. Then you can include them in your email list.

Here is the start of my email list.

Here is the start of my speaking opportunities:

Here is the start of my radio and television interview list.

Here is the start of my newspaper and magazine publicity list.

Decide on a Way to Accept Payment

You will need to decide if you will use both **credit cards** and **PayPal** for your blog. Another consideration is what type of payment, other than cash, you will accept when you are selling books face to face. I recently enrolled with **"Square"** and am pleased. I've talked to other authors who have used this and are also pleased.

"Square" is a small credit card scanner which attaches to your iPhone or Android cell phone so you can scan credit cards. The card reader itself is free. You can register for it on line at www.squareup.com. They collect your information and send you the reader. They will charge you a straight percentage for each time you use it. At this writing it is 2.75%. Go to YouTube, search for "square" and watch the video regarding its use.

Television Opportunities

TV is the toughest nut to crack, however, there are opportunities. Producers are always looking for news and timely shows.

When I worked as a publisher's marketing director I spent time building relationships with the contact people at a variety of shows. It was pretty exciting when the editor of *The Today Show* called and left a voice mail regarding one of my authors. I have also had a personal call from one of the commentators on an interview show. Just keep telling yourself that they need news as much as you need the opportunity to talk about your book or your expertise. Can you tie your book into a newsworthy event?

Before you interview on television, practice interviewing on the radio to hone your interview skills. Get ready for the unexpected questions. Learn how to speak clearly and concisely. Most radio interviews are recorded so you can listen to yourself. Determine flaws and how to correct them. Listen to other radio interviews.

Radio Shows

I found radio to be an easier nut to crack. Radio shows are constantly looking for guests. Match your expertise with the show. Call radio stations in your area to inquire about guest appearances.

I especially liked using the first two sites listed below for perusing topics and shows for my authors. Go to these sites and get on their email lists. These emails arrive daily describing radio shows that are looking for guests. The shows have both large and small audiences. Some are web radio stations with about 100 listeners. Even if you have a small audience, you should be excited to practice your radio skills.

When I found a show whose guest requirements matched one of my authors, I sent a short pitch letter. Most of the shows asked to be contacted by email. I often sent a complete press kit (see the next chapter.) which included 10 interview questions with answers.

When you are a guest, remember to tell the audience how they can purchase your book. Do an Internet search for the subject "How to Interview". While you are talking have a few note cards in front of you outlining points you would like to get across. Remember, you can interview in the living room wearing your pajamas.

The three radio show websites I've found exceptionally helpful are:

1. www.RadioGuestList.com
2. www.ReporterConnection.com
3. www.helpareporter.com   (This site also has other media opportunities.)

Radio shows I have contacted:

- _____

- _____

- _____

- _____

- _____

Speaking Opportunities

When you start out, you will most probably speak for no fee. This sounds better than saying you are free.

For authors, even though you might speak for no fee you are usually given an opportunity to sell your books. Often, you will receive room, meals and mileage. You might be promoted through their website or blog. You can also give attendees at your presentation a deal which they can collect by going to your blog or website.

When you begin your speaking career, research the opportunities in your backyard. Take out the phonebook and look for places you might speak.

I live in a large community with 1700 activities happening each month. That is one of the first places I would investigate. All of our activities are listed in our community paper with the name, phone number and email address of the leader. This is where you start cold calling, something I had to do when I sold real estate.

Again, there are books on how to make cold calls and how to approach people if you are nervous. Another method would be to send a pitch letter to the leader of the group and attach a press kit. This might not be as unnerving as cold calling.

Here are some ideas for speaking engagements:
- Clubs in the area
- Book clubs in the area
- Service clubs such as Lions, Rotary, etc.
- Conferences and conventions
- The local library
- Literary Festivals
    1. www.bookfestivals.com
    2. www.floridafairsandfestivals.com
    3. www.bibliobuffet.com
    4. www.readfest.org
    5. www.mylakelibrary.org/festival_of_reading/
    6. Do an Internet search for "Book Festivals" for more sites
- The local independent book store
- Colleges
- Public and private schools
- Companies that are associated with the theme of the book. If you have a book on banking you might look at banks, investment firms, etc.

If you write books for children, talk to the *Title 1* person in your neighboring school district. When I ran *Title 1* in Michigan, I had to plan two all-school evening activities that included families. Every year I would book an author or an illustrator. They had wonderful programs and I had state money that I had to use for these activities. I would allow my authors to sell their books.

Every Title 1 school has a parent component. It is common for schools to use parent-involvement dollars for Family Reading Night or Literacy Night. Send your press kit to the Title 1 Director of the school district. Gear your pitch letter to benefit children and parents and be sure you have a clear academic purpose for your activity. You might focus your topic on the educational literacy goals listed on the state education sites.

Also, network, network, network. When you have a speaking engagement, ask the audience if they know of any more speaker opportunities. I hand out my own speaker evaluation forms at presentations. Make sure you have a space for future engagements. Let the audience know that you would be interested in their suggestions. Also, let your friends, relatives and acquaintances know that you are a speaker. Ask for their referrals.

Now it's your turn. List 5 places you can contact for a speaking engagement. After each name tell whether you will contact by phone or email and the name of the contact person.

- _____   _____
- _____   _____
- _____   _____
- _____   _____
- _____   _____

Be sure to send a thank you note.

Decide on Your Distribution

If you are self-published, your distribution will be more limited than if you are published by a tradition house. These publishers—major houses or independents—will have distribution set up and you will only need to supplement this.

If you are self-published you most probably will have your books on Amazon, Barnes and Nobles.com, your own website and independent booksellers both brick and on-line. You also need to consider having e-book versions that are necessary in today's world. The business of e-books is exploding.

Places I can distribute my books are:

- _____
- _____
- _____
- _____
- _____

Ask for Endorsements

Give your galleys or a printed copy of your book to people you would like to endorse your book.. You can put this endorsement on the back of your book, inside, on the cover and on your blog. You can also use endorsements in videos and in your newsletter. I have known people who have sent their books to a major writer or speaker and asked them to write an endorsement. Don't be afraid. Go after people with good credentials and who are well known in your field.

People I will ask for an endorsement are:

- _____
- _____
- _____
- _____
- _____

Send Your Galleys to Reviewers

I have included a list of major reviewers for you. You need to go to their websites and peruse their requirements. Most major reviewers want galleys sent to them 3-4 months before the publication date. I believe it is well worth the effort to have your book reviewed by a major reviewer. Many of these reviews are read by people who order books, such as librarians.

The reviewers I will send to are:

- _____
- _____
- _____
- _____
- _____

Be sure to send a cover letter with your galley. Write your pitch letter to target the reviewer. Check the pitch letter and press release in "Month Three" of this book. If you decide to send to early reviewers write those two pieces now.

If you develop separate letters for reviewers outside the press/media kit, include these facts:

- Name of the book
- Publisher
- ISBN Number
- The length of the book
- The price
- Release date
- A short summary

You can even put a check form on the bottom of your letter asking them to return the information. Or you could use a postcard. The post card could have the printed form on one side and a picture of your book on the front side. The form can say something like:

- We will review this book on _____ (approximate date).
- Please send author photo. _____
- This book does not meet our needs at this time. _____

Start Blogging on Blog Sites with Themes Connected to Your Book

Okay, you have found the blogs with themes connected to your book. Now it is time to make your presence known. Do an Internet search for "author blog tour" and you will get sites that will perform a booking service for you. One such site is www.authorblogtours.com. At this writing I believe they are charging $95.00 to hook you up with bloggers for tours. There are also other sites you can check out.

So, what is a blog tour and why do you want one or two or three? A blog tour is a speaking opportunity that you are doing on-line. I told my authors they could go to the public library or bookstore and speak before 50 people, or go on-line and speak to a potentially larger audience. If a blog is a good one and has 500 followers, you have an opportunity to speak before all 500. Set a specific time that you will "chat" with followers. Do some pre-work so that the followers know information about you and your book. Show up that day and "chat" with people on the blog.

You can book blog tours yourself. One good way is with the author affiliation you have built. Look at the audience of these blogs and see what tours might be appropriate. You can book each other for blog tours.

The marketing book *Plug Your Book* by Steve Weber gives a very practical example of a blog tour and how to approach bloggers to ask them to host you. You should read the chapter "Blog Tours" (pgs. 87-96 of *Plug Your Book*) for some good information. As you continue blogging with your favorite sites, they will get to know you and trust you. Remember, you are making your presence known.

Notes

Month Three—Time for a Press/Media Kit

You're almost there!

Check List

- Develop your letterhead stationery and matching business cards (2)

- Develop your signature on your emails

- Develop your press kit (1)

- Create a "Speakers Page" (3)

- _____

- _____

Develop Your Letter head Stationary and Business Cards

When I worked for a small publisher, I developed letter head stationary on my computer using the company logo. Our business cards were developed through www.vista.com. Make sure the cards and stationary match.

I printed my mailing labels using Avery Labels. Their print software is free online. I used larger mailing labels and inserted a picture of our logo on all the labels. I believe that is a nice touch. You can also insert a picture of your book cover.

Whatever method you choose, make sure your stationary, business cards and mailers look very professional. Use heavy weight paper with a good black ink cartridge.

Develop the Signature on Your Emails

Put a "signature" at the end of each of your emails. For example, this could be the signature that I would sign each email with:

Linda terBurg
lindaterburg@gmail.com
Marketing and Promoting Your Book
Author of *The Incredible Book Launch: A Do-It-Yourself Marketing Plan Workbook*

My email carrier is Gmail. When I pull up my email there is a small picture of a gear on the right hand corner. Clicking on the gear will get a set of options. Clicking on "settings" will take me to a page where I find "signature". I have two choices. I can choose "no signature" or I can choose to add a signature. I write the signature I wish in the box. Every email I send will automatically end with the "signature" I have written.

You should put your name, the name of your book, your email address and perhaps your phone number. You can even put a quote from your book. Or a short endorsement. You can change your signature as often as seems necessary.

Here is what my email signature will comprise of:

- My name _____
- The name of my book(s) _____
- A quote from my book _____
- An endorsement _____
- A way to contact me _____

You don't need to have all of these elements. Use the ones which fit with your book(s). Don't get too lengthy.

Develop Your Press Kit

You need a professional press kit to send to TV shows, radio shows and speaking engagements. This is a packet of information about you and your book. You can also use it when requesting blog tours, on your social media sites and for submitting to press release websites. This is a very important part of your marketing plan. You can send the press kit both electronically and through snail mail. It will deliver a polished professional image about you and your book.

There are 5 major pieces of your press kit. These are:

- The pitch letter
- The press release
- The author bio
- A picture of your book's front cover.
- A list of 10 talking questions with answers

How to Display Your Press/Media Kit

- Copy your pages on good stationary. I often used stationary I bought at Wal-Mart for this. The paper was by Southworth, the Connoisseur Collection, 24 lb. I used the ivory.

- Put your 5 papers in a good quality pocket folder. You can even have folders custom made on-line if you care to spend the money. They are beautiful, but could cost around $300 to $500 for these folders. These folders might have a picture of the cover of your book on the front. Or a saying from one of the characters. Make sure the folders you buy have a slot on the inside pocket for your business card. You can compare sites by doing an Internet search for "custom folders." Three sites I have found are:
    - www.thefolderstore.com,
    - www.officedepot.com, and
    - www.4imprint.com.

- Fold the papers at different intervals and stagger them so you can clearly see there are five letterheads in the folder. I would put the pitch letter on the left hand side folded so that the editor can clearly see that this is intended for her/him.

- Use a good mailing envelope if you are sending this snail mail. I also printed out the address on a large Avery label that includes the company logo or a picture of the book cover.

- Above all ... BE PROFESSIONAL.

The Pitch Letter

This is the first thing an editor should see. It should grab the editor's attention with a quick fact, a question or a hook. You are telling the editor why they might want to book you. Or why they might want to promote your book. You are "pitching" your case to the editor.

Be sure to change each pitch letter to target the editor to whom you are sending it. End your pitch letter with a request. It is the action you wish the editor to take. Let the editor know how this action will benefit him/her. Always remember the WIIFM: **What's In It For Me?**

On the next page is a copy of a pitch letter. It is one we used for a book about Alzheimer's from one of my authors.

Fireside Publications, Inc.
www.firesidepubs.com
Linda A. terBurg, Marketing Director
352-751-1000

ABC Show
NY, NY

Dear editor (insert name),

….40, 50, 60, 68 seconds. Someone new in the U.S. has just developed Alzheimer's disease. Has it touched your life yet? As the Baby Boomer generation continues to grow older, the episodes of Alzheimer's increases significantly.

In her newly released book, *Essays: On Living with Alzheimer's Disease: The First Twelve Months*, Dr. Lois Bennett gives an intimate look at living with AD from three viewpoints. Not only has she been diagnosed with AD, but she discusses this disease from her roles as caretaker to her mother and practicing psychologist.

Become privy to the intimate feelings of the author as she watches loved ones suffer and then has the dreaded diagnosis applied to her own life in a rather bizarre way. Feel her strength as she does not allow herself to become a victim and gives practical ways for patients to enrich their lives through lifestyle changes.

A short version of the first chapter can also be found in *Chicken Soup for the Soul: Thinking Positive*, available in major bookstores after September 27, 2010.

Please have this dynamic, well-researched guest on your show. Her courage, knowledge and strength will enrich your viewing audience.

Sincerely,

Linda terBurg
Marketing Director
Fireside Publications
www.firesidepubs.com
terburg@comcast.net

The Press Release

The press release is also on one sheet of letterhead paper. It will include:

- The contact person
- The book name
- The ISBN Number
- Whether it is paperback, eBook, etc.
- The price
- The number of pages
- The release date
- The book category

Use the press release when you release your book. You can also have press releases to alert members of the news media to book signings, speaking engagements, or any other newsworthy event. Announce a new product included with you book. You could announce a climb in book sales. Again, I always include the press release when I am pitching an editor or news person. If you want to send out multiple press releases, you can hire a press releasing service. Do an Internet search for "press release" and find a multitude of services you can explore.

<u>Three such services are</u>:

- PR Web (www.prweb.com) This service has a cost
- PR Newswire (www.prnewswire.com) This service has a cost.
- PR Log (www.prlog.org) At this writing, this service has a free aspect. They also have varying prices depending on a variety of news aspects.

On the next page is a copy of a press release we used on the same book.

Fireside Publications, Inc.
www.firesidepubs.com
Linda A. terBurg, Marketing Director
352-751-1000

PRESS RELEASE

For additional information, please contact:
Linda terBurg
Marketing Director
Fireside Publications
Firesidepubs1@comcast.net

ESSAYS ON LIVING WITH ALZHEIMER'S DISEASE: THE FIRST TWELVE MONTHS
By Lois Wilmoth-Bennett, Ph.D.
ISBN: 978-1-935517-07-8
Trade paper, 140 pages, $15.98
October, 2010
Non-Fiction, Health, Illness

This book shares an overview of scientific and historical data, along with personal experiences of the author, a psychologist, in becoming a caregiver and ultimately a patient. Become privy to the intimate feelings of the author as she watches loved ones suffer and then has the dreaded diagnosis applied to her own life in a rather bizarre way. Share her feelings as she makes the decision to not become a victim—to do what she can to slow the process then to get on with her life. Find about what comes next after the diagnosis; read about steps the author has taken to adjust and perhaps extend her mental functioning a bit longer.

Learn about the statistics of Alzheimer's disease and the incidence level. It will be impossible to escape it's affect on family, friends or even yourself, as it reaches epidemic proportions in the near future. Every 70 seconds, someone develops AD. By mid-century, scientists predict the incidence will increase to one every 33 seconds.

Read the heartfelt poetry by Colett Sasina in the chapter "Dementia in Verse." Ms. Sasina brings out the innermost feelings of humankind, emotions both happy and sad, with a tad of humor along the way.

"Prepare to enter the mind of a brilliant professional who has chosen to share her recent journey .... Her words can help others with an AD diagnosis. Her words can help families who have loved ones diagnosed with AD. Her words can help other professionals learn from her experience." From Forward, Richard H. Kiley, Ph.D, Licensed Psychologist, Executive Director of the Appalachian Community Health Center

The Author Bio and Picture

This should also be one page long and on logo stationary with your picture. When I had a small budget, I copied the pictures of my authors from their book covers. One author sent me large glossies to use in his press kit. These can be used for the snail mail kit. You will also need a picture that you can include in the electronic version.

Be sure your biography is interesting and includes facts that show you are the expert. You may include such things as your expertise, facts about any books released and information on how to contact you or your web page/blog. Also, list literary contests and awards won and professional writing organizations you belong to.

Don't get too wordy. This should be a brief capsule to give the editor a quick glimpse of you and your accomplishments. You can even gear your bio to the book you are pitching. Start the first paragraph with facts relating to your current project.

On the next page is an example of an author bio.

MARK H. NEWHOUSE
Marknewhousebooks.com
1042 Sayle St. Lady Lake, FL 32162

The Author's Guild   telephone
SCBWI   email mark@newhouse.net
The Florida Writers Association   blog: marknewhouse.blogspot.com

BIOGRAPHY: Mark H. Newhouse

Mark H. Newhouse is an award winning-teacher and author. Born in Germany to Holocaust survivors, he loved teaching in Central Islip, New York, and as an adjunct education professor at SUNY Old Westbury. He was named Elementary/Secondary Teacher of the Year (NYS Reading Assoc., 1989).

Mark's passions for children, education and humor earned *The Rockhound Science Mysteries, Learning Magazine's Teachers' Choice Award, 2001. You Never See Fat Vampires*, (Court Jester Publications), about bullying, won First Prize, Florida Writers Association 2011, YA published fiction. *Alice in Transylvania* won First Prize for unpublished picture book, 2011. *Who Killed Mr. Bulk?* took 3rd place unpublished middle grade fiction 2010. In addition, Mark has won various awards for his short stories.

Mark is the founder/leader of the Children's Author Team, contributor and Editor-in-Chief for *The Story Shop* and *Holiday Helpings* (Court Jester Publications). Other books include *Who's Afraid of Essays?* (Earthkids Publishing), and *Unforgettable at Any Speed* (Quixote Press)

Mark received his BA and MA from Queens College, New York and resides in Florida where he is the founding President of The Writers League of The Villages with almost two hundred members. Mark's books are available from Amazon.com, B&N.com, marknewhousebooks.com and other outlets. Contact him directly for Skype and personal appearances.

The Book Cover

Include a picture of the book cover on the letterhead stationery. You might want to include the back cover, also.

This is an example of the book cover on the letterhead stationary:

Fireside Publications, Inc.
www.firesidepubs.com
Linda A. terBurg, Marketing Director
352-751-1000

A List of Ten Questions with Answers:

Prepare ten questions with short answers to help interviewers. When I received an interview for my authors, if possible, I made sure the host had the book in plenty of time to read before the interview. Sometimes, I had the authors prepare a list of 5 talking topics, too. Try to keep your questions and answers to one page. Think of questions that your audience might ask you. Practice the tough questions, too. You will have to know how to answer them when you are interviewed.

Here is an example of Ten Questions with Answers on letterhead stationary:

Mary Lois Sanders, Author
mary.lois.sanders@att.net
7043 SE 17rd Arlington Loop, The Villages, FL 32162

Questions that can be used in interviews:

Q. You write and publish *Creative Writer's Notebook*, a newsletter for writers. Do you consider yourself an expert in teaching others to write?
A. Expert? No. Knowledgeable, yes. I've been writing professionally for over 25 years and editing for 20 and I've learned a lot. I read about writing, attend workshops and conferences, and am a member of several writers' critique groups. Part of writing about writing is knowing whom to interview and what books to research.

Q. How did you get into writing?
A. In high school, my most obvious talent was singing, so I majored in music in college. However, I never let go of the dream of creative writing. I began writing Bible study curriculum for children and then branched out to the secular market with articles and short stories for children's magazines. The next step was writing novels.

Q. Some believe writing for children is easier than writing for adults. Is this true?
A. Far from it. You must know childhood development, reading levels, vocabulary, sentence structure for each age group. And of course, you need to know what the kids like to read. Young children like to hear stories, or read them, about other children their own age. Middle graders like to read "up", e.g., a 9-10 year old likes to read about main characters who are older, but not too much. Young teens like to read about older teens. All genres apply for middle grade and YAs, too. Writers must choose what age group they want to target before they begin a project.

Q. So, what are these different targets?
A. *Beginning with the youngest target, we have Picture Books (2months to 8 years); Story Books (6-8 years); Chapter Books (2nd - 4th Grades); Middle grade novels (4th - 7th grades); and YA novels (6th - 9th grades). Older teens often read adult books and what we call cross-overs like the Twilight Series.*

Q. Why did you choose to write historical fiction for middle grade children?
A. *I loved historical fiction as a child and that's still one of my favorite genres. Historical novels help children learn and understand about how people lived and worked. Teachers also like novels they can recommend that travel right along with the curriculum they are teaching. Makes a good market.*

Q. What makes a book historical fiction?
A. *The historical setting has to be an integral part of the story. Gone With the Wind is a good example. My novel, The Spirit Journey of Timothy Michael O'Hara, is another. Without the setting and historical events, the characters have no story.*

Q. How do you choose the historical background for your novels?
A. *I read and we travel. I also like maps. When my husband and I moved to New Jersey I looked at a map and found Washington-Crossing-the-Delaware State Park. What a great place to start!*

Q. So Historical fiction takes a lot of research.
A. *True, but you never use every bit of information you learn. You don't want your novel to read like a history book! And books set today need research, too.*

Q. As a woman, do you find it difficult to develop a story with a Main Character who is a boy?
A. *No. I recognized that I needed input from guys to make sure I wasn't giving my MC what they would consider "female" reactions and dialogue. Having good readers is a must for any writer!*

Q. Tell us the title of your book, and where it may be bought.
A. The Spirit Journey of Timothy Michael O'Hara* *may be purchased at major bookstores, on-line from Great Major Book Publishing or Amazon.com. It is also available on Amazon Kindle.*

* Actually, this book is headed to my agent for marketing to publishers!

Notes

Month Two—A Bit of Everything

Work with Video Sites, Blogging and Lists

Check List

- _____Place your book trailer on video sites (3)

- _____Place your first of 10 videos on video sharing sites

- _____Keep your blogging going with sites related to your book (1)

- _____Solicit radio and television shows for guest appearances

- _____Contact speaker opportunities (2)

- _____

- _____

Get Your Book Trailer and Videos on Video Sharing Sites

You should have your book trailer finished by now and at least the first of your 10 videos. Start uploading them to the video sharing sites listed in this book. I believe it is important to start with YouTube. Work your way through other sites that could be beneficial for your book.

Keep Your Blogging Going

By now you have found your blogging sites and have been blogging on a regular basis. You can determine how much time you would like to devote to this activity. Are you going to blog 30 minutes a day, 30 minutes every other day or 2 times a week for 30 minutes? Try to be consistent so that people expect your presence.

Start Contacting Television Shows, Radio Shows, Opportunities for Speaking Engagements and Book Signings

Now is the time to contact people to arrange appearances and speaking opportunities.

- Keep a good record of whom you have contacted and when you sent your press kit.
- Make a personal call about 5-7 days after they have received your written pitch.
- Keep records. I use a spreadsheet.

Make it easy for people to have you speak. Write the script for the television or radio show and send it to them. Think about your angle when you write this.

If you are doing a book signing, plan a 15-20 minute interactive talk which will precede the signing.

- Ask the store to set up chairs with a small table at the front of the chairs.
- Have refreshments for the customers. A bookstore in Michigan where I lived always had free coffee, cookies and water for the fans. If they don't provide this, ask if you can provide this yourself.
- Don't sit down at your table. Mingle with the fans or walk around the bookstore.
- Be sure to wear a badge with your name and "AUTHOR" printed under your name.

As you read passages from your book, ask people to turn to the page you are reading. It will necessitate that they are holding your book. Let them know that you welcome questions at any point. At the end, ask for questions. If they are slow to respond you might say, "I'm always asked this question." And then answer it. Get the ball rolling.

Be sure you are ready to speak on camera, on the radio or before a group of live customers. There is nothing better than rehearsal, rehearsal, rehearsal!

- _____Find a partner and rehearse your questions and answers

- _____Practice for the length of your segment. (Be sure to ask how long you have.)
- _____If you are not sure of an answer, repeat the question to stall. Or say something like "that's a good question."
- _____If you are asked a negative question, always answer in the positive.
- _____**Most important**. Repeat the name of your book and where to find it.

Notes

Month One—Create Anticipation and Excitement

Check List

- _____ Develop your first newsletter (2)

- _____ Get bookmarks and any promotional materials printed

- _____ Ask blog sites if you can have a Blog Tour (3)

- _____ Set up your Facebook Fan Page for your book (1)

- _____ Are you still reading?

- _____

- _____

- _____

Develop Your First Newsletter

What is the one thing everybody seems to do many times during the day? Check their inbox. You need to take advantage of this universal phenomenon. Develop a newsletter, get into the inbox, get the newsletter opened and move your customers to action.

When I worked for a publishing company I sent out one or two newsletters on a monthly basis. Be consistent so people don't forget you. But don't be a pest either. I tried to keep the letters newsy and a bit homey. I had a conversation with each customer. I also gave tips on the publishing business and offered contests.

I used Constant Contact (www.constantcontact.com) which is an email marketing program. It is easy to use and you can track the progress of the newsletters you send out. I had about 500 customers on my email list. After my newsletter went out, I could go to the tracking program and see who had opened my emails, who had forwarded my emails and who went to my webpage. I also knew if they went more than once. This is a very affordable program and you can start with a free email newsletter campaign.

Since I began using this program, they have started featuring a "social campaign" which interfaces with your Facebook Page. This program is also free and they offer a lot of help in running this kind of campaign.

Another email campaign program is www.mailchimp.com. I have not used this, but it, too, looks affordable and offers a tracking program. Check this out, too.

This is where you begin using all the email addresses you have collected. You will enter them in a program at Constant Contact. You can make many different lists and just send a particular newsletter to the people in list 1 and list 2. Maybe that is where you put your *Romance Fans*. Maybe you also have a book on *Dating*. You could have an entirely different list for these fans. Or maybe your newsletter is meant for everyone so you send it to all of your lists.

I believe it is important to keep your customers updated and a professional newsletter does this beautifully. This is a great marketing tool. **Get into the inbox.**

Get Promotional Material Printed

You can get lots of promotional materials printed for your book. Again, it just depends on how much you want to spend, your goals and what you are going to do with them. Most of my authors had bookmarks printed. Some had posters of the book printed and some had postcards printed. You need to determine how you will use these. My personal feeling is to start with a few printed materials. You might want to hand these out during a speaking engagement, or a book signing. I would start small and see where it goes.

Ask Blog Sites if You can Have a Blog Tour

You've been blogging for three months now. Plus you have read everything you can about how to conduct a blog tour. Now it is time to begin asking blog sites if you can have a blog tour. Use all the social etiquette you can when approaching blogs hosts. Make sure you thank them for their hospitality and make yourself a good guest.

I have asked these sites to conduct a blog tour:

- _____
- _____
- _____
- _____
- _____

Set up the Facebook Fan Page for Your Book

Now is the time to publish your fan page.
  A. Scroll down to the bottom of your wall
  B. Click on "create a page"
  C. Click on the box that says "Artist, Band or Public Figure"
  D. Choose a category "Author"
  E. Write in the name of your book
  F. Agree to their terms by checking the box
  G. Get started
  H. Upload your profile picture. Use the cover of your book.
  I. Follow the directions on the screen. You can invite all of your email buddies and facebook friends to follow your page. Facebook will walk you through this.

Are You Still Reading?

Be sure you are still reading marketing materials. You can do this with books or by doing an Internet search of marketing subjects. There are a lot of free book marketing materials on the Internet. But keep reading.

At Publication Date

WOOHOO!
YOU DID IT YOURSELF!

Check List

- _____Send out your first newsletter announcing the publication of your book (1)

- _____Have an open house and invite all the people who have supported you and those on your email lists. Invite the local press. Instead of a book signing, hand our book labels with a picture of your book and your signature. (2)

- _____Send out press releases before the open house to your local newspapers, radio, and TV stations. This is the start of using your media/press kit. (3)

- _____Ask the Amazon top reviewers to review you book

- _____Ask your followers to write reviews for your book. You could even give them a free book or a free eBook.

- _____Enter contests

- _____Consider joining Amazon Prime

- _____Spend a day enhancing all of your pages on Amazon, Facebook, Twitter, LinkedIn and Pinterest.

- _____Sign up for Kindlegraph

- _____

- _____

Send out Your First Newsletter Announcing the Publication of Your Book

Now it's time for your first newsletter. You have signed up for your newsletter program and have entered the emails of your customers into the program. You have played around with the templates and even sent one or two practice ones to yourself and your mother. It's time to perfect the announcement and send it to fans, friends and customers.

Have an Open House

Celebrate, celebrate, celebrate! If your home is large enough, have the celebration there. Give a time range. Most people won't stay for the whole time. If you are shy about asking people to come and buy your book, let them know that no books will be sold at the open house. Serve refreshments and decorate.

If you go with "no books sold", I suggest printing name plates which you will hand out. You can buy fancy ones and print them yourself. You should have a picture of the book printed in color and your signature. You can even write something catchy above your name. Let people know they are getting these so they can put them into your book when they buy it.

This is also a good time to have printed material available. Some ideas are:

- A large poster of your book cover
- Bookmarks
- Postcards
- Wear a T-shirt with a picture of your book cover

Start listing people you will invite. Invite the local press, too.

People I will invite to my open house:

- _____
- _____
- _____

Send out Press Releases

Send your press releases to the local newspaper and radio station about a week or two before the open house. Follow up with a phone call. Invite your local reporters to the open house. Maybe they could cover the release of your book at the open house?

If you go with a press release service there is usually a yearly charge. One company, PRBuzz, will distribute your press releases all year for $299 for a single company. You can also team up with your affiliate authors and buy a subscription for $499. Any time you have a speaking engagement or a book signing send out a press release. Your Google Alert should pick up your release in the internet so you will get a copy, too.

Places I will send my press release to are:

- _____
- _____
- _____
- _____
- _____
- _____

Ask the Amazon Top Reviewers to Read and Review Your Book

Go to www.amazon.com/review/top-reviewers and search through the list of top reviewers. Read each one's profile, get a feel for how they write a review and see what kinds of books interest them. When you find a reviewer with interests matching your book, send them an email and ask for a review.

Amazon Top Reviewers I might contact are:

- _____
- _____
- _____
- _____
- _____

Ask Your Followers/Customers to Write a Review and Post it on Amazon

Ask anyone who has read your book to write a review on Amazon. Ask for a review on your printed bookmarks. Give your fans a printed bookmark that should tweak their memory to write that review.

People I can ask to write reviews are:

- _____
- _____
- _____
- _____
- _____
- _____
- _____

Enter Contests

Now is the time to investigate entering your book in a contest or two. Explore these contests and find a match for your book. Do an Internet search for "writing contests" and you will find more. Also, the newsletter by Mary Lois Sanders included in the reading list of this book is a necessary tool. She does a good job of listing contests each month. It's a great bang for your buck and you'll get an issue monthly.

Contests and Awards:

1. Boston Globe—**Horn Book Awards**. For children's books. For fiction, non-fiction, picture book. http://www.hbook.com

2. **Alex Award.** Given yearly to 10 books written for adults which can be cross-over books for young adults ages 12-18. www.ala.org/yalsa/booklists/alex

3. **Christopher Awards.** Books for young people. http://www.christophers.org

4. **Golden Kite Award,** for members of SCBWI. http://scbwi.org

5. **Sophie Brody Award** to encourage, recognize and commend outstanding achievement in Jewish Literature. www.ala.org/rusa/awards/brody

6. **Scott O'Dell Award.** Given for distinguished work of historical fiction for children or young adults. www.scottodell.com

7. **William Sanders Scarborough Prize.** Award for an outstanding scholarly study of African-American literature or culture published the previous year. http://www.mla.org/prizeinfo_wss

8. **John Newbery Award.** http://ala.org. "This award is the most prestigious children's book award that an author can receive."

9. **National Jewish Book Council.** http://www.jewishbookcouncil.org

10. **The Children's Book Committee.** Selects 600 titles for inclusion in *The Best Children's Books of the Year*. www.bnkst.edu/center-childrens-literature/

11. **Royal Palm Literary Award.** This is given by the Florida Writers Association each year. There are a variety of categories. You can join this association and enter your book even if you do not live in Florida. You just have to become a member and pay your dues. www.floridawriters.net

12. Check the *Writer's Market* and *The Creative Writer's Notebook* for other contests and awards.

13. **CIPA EVVY Awards** by the Colorado Independent Publishers Association (CIPA). If you don't live in Colorado you can still get an affiliate membership for $55.00 and enter the contest. www.cipacatalog.com/

14. **Pulitzer Prize**. Did you know that you can nominate your own book? You can. Go to www.pulitzer.org to read the guidelines. Your book must be published in the year you enter, i.e., books published in 2012 are eligible for the 2012 Pulitzer Prize. The book may be hardcover or bound paperback. The author must be a U.S. citizen, except in the history category.

15. **John Esten Cooke Fiction Award**. Given annually to encourage writers of Southern History to portrait history in an accurate manner.

16. Are you an editor? Did a book you edited get an award? Let people know. Put it in your media kit.

Contests I will enter:

- _____

- _____

- _____

- _____

Consider Joining Amazon Prime

Amazon has a lending program called Prime. They lend books to prime members who pay for a membership. An Amazon Prime member can borrow one book per month free of charge from a list of books in the program. You can put your eBook in the program. To find out more about this program, go to: www.kdp.amazon.com/selfpublishing/KDPselect

There is research on the Internet that says authors have gotten good returns from putting their books into the Prime program. Some say that they have gotten many sales after the book has been lent in the program. Some also say that it helps the sales of their other books.

One way you can verify this is by checking your overall Amazon ranking before and after your book has been lent for a day. This ranking is in the overall statistics. You should also check your rating after a big speaking engagement. This is one way you can track sales by your efforts.

Spend a Day Enhancing All of Your Pages on Facebook, Twitter, LinkedIn and Amazon

- _____Go to Facebook and update any information on your personal page and your Fan Page

- _____Go to Twitter and update any personal information.

- _____Go to LinkedIn and update any personal information

- _____Go to Pinterest and update any personal information

- _____Go to Amazon and enhance your page. Check such things as:

1. _____Your Book Cover

2. _____Show the table of contents

3. _____Look over your reviews. Should you ask for more?

4. _____Are you showing excerpts?

5. _____Your author information. Is it compelling?

Sign up for Kindlegraph

According to its website (www.kindlegraph.com), *Kindlegraph* is a service that "enables authors to sign e-books for their readers. It can be personalized to the reader. Requesting, sending and receiving *Kindlegraphs* is free. If a reader uses Amazon's Personal Document Service to receive a *Kindlegraph* on his/her Kindle, then Amazon may charge a small delivery fee. *Kindlegraph* earns an affiliate fee for any books purchased from Amazon.com after clicking on one of the Amazon links on Kindlegraph.com."

A unique part of *Kindlegraph* is that it actually draws the signature. The reader can collect these signatures on his/her Kindle. The reader can also ask for signatures on hardcover and paperback books.

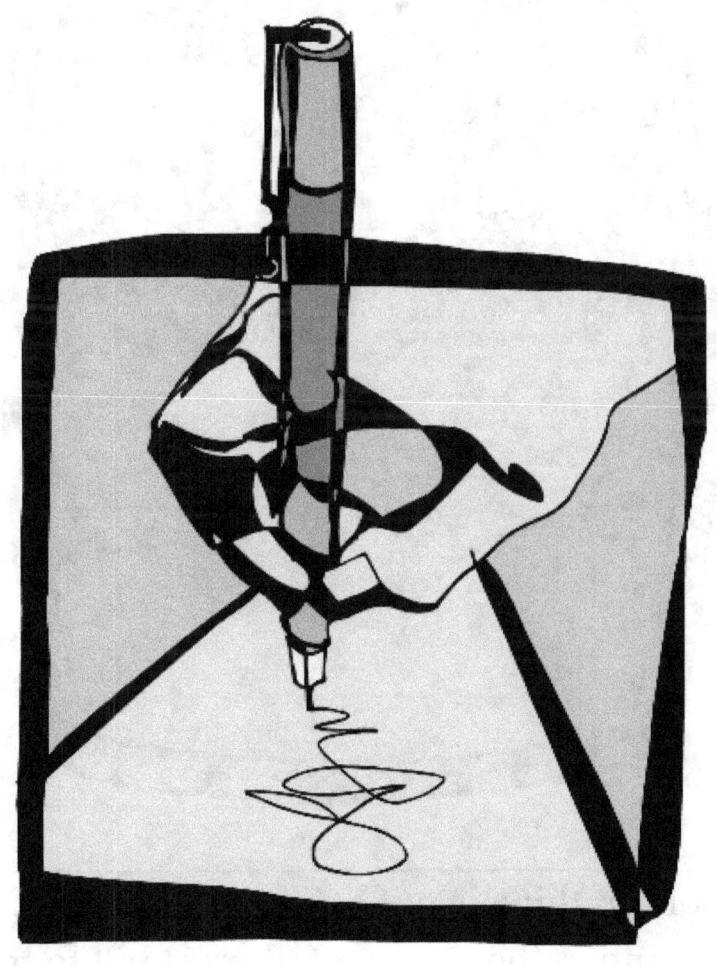

Now What?

You are an entrepreneur. You must continue with your marketing efforts. Even if you are writing the sequel or the next sequel, you must devote the time to marketing.

If you have started a Master Mind Group, continue with your planning focusing on goal setting. Be sure to determine how much time you will devote daily or weekly to your marketing effort.

Good luck. My hopes are that you fulfill all of your dreams of becoming a well publicized author with a fabulous following.

"The important thing is not being afraid to take a chance. Remember, the greatest failure is not to try."
—Debbie Fields, Founder Mrs. Fields Cookies

Appendix - Calendars

Note: The first 10 calendars are examples. The 11th calendar is blank and may be reproduced as often as needed.

Month Nine: March

Sun	Mon	Tues	Wed	Thu	Fri	Sat
	Start Reading Marketing Books					
	Read					
	Read					
	Read					
	Read					

Notes:

Month Eight: April

Sun	Mon	Tues	Wed	Thu	Fri	Sat
	Become an expert					
	Work on developing my expert ideas					
	Write Expert Articles Write at least two to start			Explore article directories	Build my blog	
	Post articles in article directories					
	Post first (Connect this to my blog)					
	Post second article (Connect this to my blog)					
	Build networks with other authors					

Month Seven: <u>May</u>

Sun	Mon	Tues	Wed	Thu	Fri	Sat
	Download *Book Marketecture*		Complete pages to determine my book's message		Complete pages to determine my book's audience	
	Develop my budget				Set up a MasterMind Group	
	Develop my goals				Order MasterMind Journals	
	Research Other Books like Mine		Read Other Books Like Mine			
	Write Reviews for Other Books Like Mine					

Notes:

Month Six: **June**

Sun	Mon	Tues	Wed	Thu	Fri	Sat
	Get on Facebook			Get on Pinterest		
	Get on Twitter		Get on LinkedIn			
	Set Up Google Alerts			Start My Book Trailer		
	Join Buffer					
				Have Book Trailer Finished		

Notes:

Month Five: <u>July</u>

Sun	Mon	Tues	Wed	Thu	Fri	Sat
	Have galleys made					
	Find blogs related to me books			Find chat rooms related to my book		
		Begin planning 1st video for sharing site				
	Start investigating video sharing sites listed in book			Investigate a video sharing site	Investigate a video sharing site	
	Investigate a video sharing site			Investigate a video sharing site		

Notes:

Month Four: <u>August</u>

Sun	Mon	Tues	Wed	Thu	Fri	Sat
	Compile TV list			Compile radio list		
	Compile email list					
	Compile speaker list				Sign up with Square	
	Decide on distribution					
	Ask for endorsements for book		Send galleys to reviewers		Start blogging on blog sites	

Notes:

Month Three: **September**

Sun	Mon	Tues	Wed	Thu	Fri	Sat
	Design and order business cards		Design matching stationary			
	Put signature on my emails				Create speaker's page	
	Develop Press Kit (PK)		Develop Pitch Letter for PK			
		Develop Press Release for PK			Develop Author Bio for PK	
	Develop 10 Question for PK			Determine Picture for PK	Print all PK pictures on Letterhead stationary	

Notes:

Month Two: **October**

Sun	Mon	Tues	Wed	Thu	Fri	Sat
	Keep blogging			Place video #1 on video sharing site		
	Place book trailer on video site			Solicit radio shows for guest appearances		
	Solicit TV shows for guest appearance					
	Contact speaker opportunities					

Notes:

Month One: <u>November</u>

Sun	Mon	Tues	Wed	Thu	Fri	Sat
	Decide on my newsletter carrier			Order bookmarks and promotional materials		
	Ask blog sites if I can have a blog tour			Ask another blog site if I can have a blog tour		
	Keep reading			Set up my Facebook Fan Page		
	Send out 1st newsletter announcing the book					

Notes:

Book Launch Date: <u>December</u>

Sun	Mon	Tues	Wed	Thu	Fri	Sat
	Send out newsletter announcing publication of the book	Send out invites to open house		Send out press releases to local TV and newspaper		
Open House			Ask Amazon top reviewers to review my book		Ask people who read my book to write reviews	
	Enter contests	Sign up for Kindlegraph			Enhance all my social media pages	

Notes:

Month Year: _____

Sun	Mon	Tues	Wed	Thu	Fri	Sat

Notes:

About the Author

Linda terBurg is an in-demand speaker and consultant for book marketing. She has worked as a Marketing Director, School Administrator, Realtor and trainer. She has trained extensively in both business and education. Besides a degree in English and Public Speaking and a Master's Degree in Education, Linda also has a Master of Business Administration with a major in Marketing. While majoring in journalism in college and reporting for her college newspaper, her first paying job was in the morgue of The Detroit News. Linda has co-edited two anthologies that also contain stories and poems she has written. She would love to hear your success stories. You can contact Linda at lindaterburg@gmail.com

www.ingramcontent.com/pod-product-compliance
Lightning Source LLC
Chambersburg PA
CBHW081238180526
45171CB00005B/458